mini-waffle

cookbook

mini-waffle
cookbook

Recipes and photography
by Lynda Balslev

Andrews McMeel
PUBLISHING®

contents

a handy-dandy pocket guide to mini waffles

Classic, trendy, versatile, adored . . . no, we are not referring to your ideal BFF. It's the next best thing: It's a waffle. Who doesn't like waffles? Whether it's good old-fashioned buttermilk waffles doused in maple syrup, down-home manwhich sloppy joes, or chocolate-coated waffle pops, waffles are a carb-lover's dream come true.

Fabulously flexible, there is a waffle for everyone. You can call waffles breakfast, lunch, dinner, and dessert. They are compatible with nearly everything—fried eggs, melted cheese, sandwich fixings, meaty burgers, fresh fruit, and ice cream—so the possibilities are virtually limitless. You can bake brownies, fry fritters, toast bread, even crisp puff pastry dough on a waffle iron. Chances are if you can press it, toast it, bake it, or panfry it, you can waffle it—which is a very good thing, because everything looks better covered in crispy little waffle squares.

So go on, stop waffling (pun intended) and get cooking. All you need is a waffle iron, your imagination, and some inspiration. There are twenty sweet and savory recipes within to make using a mini-waffle iron along with a few basic tips to ensure waffle success.

waffles 101

INGREDIENTS

Flour power: Not too heavy, not too light, unbleached all-purpose flour is just right.

Got milk? The fat in whole milk keeps waffles light. When using buttermilk, add baking soda to the dry ingredients. It will react with buttermilk's natural acidity and boost the leavening you need for a lighter waffle.

Keep 'em light: Try separating your eggs to lighten up your waffles. Mix the yolk into the batter and whip the egg white until light and fluffy. Gently fold the white into the batter without overmixing.

COOKING TIPS

- Bring all of your ingredients to room temperature before mixing.
- Do not overmix the batter—a little lumpiness is OK!
- No peeking: The waffles are cooked when the iron stops steaming. Do not lift the lid until the steaming stops.
- Remove the waffle from the iron with a silicone utensil to avoid scratching the nonstick surface.

- Place the waffle on a wire rack to cool slightly (if you can wait) to prevent sogginess from the residual heat.
- When making a large batch, place the waffles, uncovered, on a baking sheet in a 200°F oven while you prepare the remaining waffles.

CREATIVE WAFFLES

Who needs bread? Waffles are a great substitute for bread in sandwiches. Use waffles fresh from the waffle maker, or prepare them in advance. To refresh, simply toast them until crisp and pile on your favorite sandwich fixings. Savory or sweet, waffles are endlessly versatile. Use the Basic Waffles (page 3) as your template, and add fruit, whole grains, nuts, chocolate chips, or even grated vegetables to the batter.

Which brings us to . . . faux-waffles: Use your waffle iron for more than just waffle batter. Use it to cook eggs, potato patties, brownies, panini, even calzones.

EXTRAS! EXTRAS!

Really? You didn't eat them all, or you made a double batch? Cool the extras, wrap them tightly with plastic wrap, and store in the refrigerator for up to four days or in the freezer for one month. Reheat and crisp waffles on a baking sheet in a 400°F oven or pop them into the toaster for a quick snack.

basics

with

waffles

basic waffles

If you must have one recipe in your waffle repertoire, this is your waffle. It's a classic and the perfect template for myriad variations. Enjoy it as is, or tweak it to your taste. For a sweeter waffle, add an extra tablespoon of sugar. For a savory waffle, omit the sugar and vanilla. It's also wonderfully forgiving when it comes to extra ingredients. Add fruit, chocolate chips, even cheese, and if you're gluten-free, simply substitute the flour with your favorite gluten-free mix.

1 cup unbleached all-purpose flour

1 tablespoon sugar

1½ teaspoons baking powder

½ teaspoon sea salt

1 cup whole milk

1 large egg, lightly beaten

2 tablespoons vegetable oil or unsalted butter, melted and cooled

½ teaspoon vanilla extract (optional)

Melted butter or nonstick cooking spray, for the waffle maker

1 Combine the flour, sugar, baking powder, and salt in a medium bowl and mix well.

2 Whisk the milk, egg, oil, and vanilla, if using, in a small bowl. Add the wet ingredients to the dry ingredients and stir to combine, without overmixing. It's OK if there are a few lumps.

3 Brush a preheated mini-waffle maker with melted butter or spray with nonstick cooking spray. Pour about ¼ cup batter into the waffle maker and cook according to the manufacturer's instructions. Remove with a silicone spatula and repeat with the remaining batter.

4 Serve warm with powdered sugar, maple syrup, or your favorite topping.

buttermilk waffles

These waffles have the unmistakable tang of buttermilk, and when accompanied with luscious maple syrup and a pad of butter, they are a breakfast standard. When you use buttermilk, it's important to add baking soda to the mix. Buttermilk doesn't have the same high fat level as whole milk, which is an important component to keeping your waffles light. The baking soda will react with the acidity of the buttermilk and give you the leavening you need. For extra lightness, we separate the eggs and whip the whites until fluffy before folding into the batter.

1 cup unbleached all-purpose flour

1 tablespoon sugar

1 teaspoon baking powder

½ teaspoon baking soda

½ teaspoon sea salt

1 cup low-fat buttermilk

1 large egg, separated

3 tablespoons unsalted butter, melted and cooled

½ teaspoon vanilla extract

Melted butter or nonstick cooking spray, for the waffle maker

1 Combine the flour, sugar, baking powder, baking soda, and salt in a medium bowl.

2 Whisk the buttermilk, egg yolk, butter, and vanilla in a small bowl. Add to the dry ingredients and stir to combine, without overmixing.

3 In a small bowl, beat the remaining egg white until frothy peaks form. Gently fold the egg white into the batter, without overmixing.

4 Brush a preheated mini-waffle maker with melted butter or spray with nonstick cooking spray. Pour about ¼ cup batter into the waffle maker and cook according to the manufacturer's instructions. Remove with a silicone spatula and repeat with the remaining batter.

5 Serve warm with powdered sugar, maple syrup, or your favorite topping.

VARIATIONS

Gluten-free Waffles: Substitute 1 cup gluten-free flour mix, such as Bob's Red Mill, for the unbleached all-purpose flour.

Savory Waffles: Omit the sugar and vanilla.

Blueberry Waffles: Stir 1 cup fresh blueberries into the finished batter.

Cinnamon Waffles: Add 1 teaspoon cinnamon to the dry ingredients.

Chocolate Chip Waffles: Stir ½ cup chocolate chips into the finished batter.

rise-and-shine
yeasted waffles

MAKES 8 MINI WAFFLES

Is there a better way to wake up in the morning, than to a fluffy bowl of waffle batter ready for the making? We think not. Thanks to the slow rise and the yeast, these overnight waffles are crisp on the outside and tender on the inside, with a slight chewiness and fragrance from the yeast. So prepare the batter for these waffles the night before you make them, and we wish you very sweet dreams.

1 cup unbleached all-purpose flour

1 teaspoon instant yeast

½ teaspoon sea salt

3 tablespoons unsalted butter

¾ cup whole milk

1 large egg, lightly beaten

2 tablespoons maple syrup or honey

½ teaspoon vanilla extract

Melted butter or nonstick cooking spray, for the waffle maker

1 Whisk the flour, yeast, and salt in a large bowl.

2 Melt the butter in a small saucepan over medium-low heat. Remove from the heat and add the milk; let stand until lukewarm.

3 Add the milk and butter, the egg, syrup, and vanilla to the dry ingredients and mix to combine. Cover with plastic wrap and refrigerate overnight.

continued

4 Brush a preheated mini-waffle maker with melted butter or spray with nonstick cooking spray. Pour about ¼ cup batter into the waffle maker and cook according to the manufacturer's instructions. Remove with a silicone spatula and repeat with the remaining batter.

5 Serve warm with your favorite toppings, maple syrup, or powdered sugar.

VARIATIONS

Savory Waffles: Substitute the syrup with 1 tablespoon sugar and omit the vanilla.

Blueberry Waffles: Pour about ¼ cup batter into the waffle maker and sprinkle with blueberries. Proceed with cooking.

vegan gluten-free waffles

MAKES 6 TO 8 MINI WAFFLES

This recipe is a great alternative to Basic, Buttermilk, and Rise-and-Shine waffles. Add aromatic coconut oil, or use a vegan butter for a more neutral flavor. Gluten-free flour blends typically contain rice flour, which adds a wonderful lightness and crispiness to these waffles.

¾ cup almond milk

1 tablespoon apple cider vinegar

1 cup gluten-free flour blend, such as Bob's Red Mill

1 teaspoon baking powder

½ teaspoon sea salt

2 tablespoons coconut oil or vegan butter, such as Earth Balance, melted and cooled

2 tablespoons maple syrup or sugar

½ teaspoon vanilla extract (optional)

Melted vegan butter or nonstick vegan cooking spray, for the waffle maker

1 Combine the almond milk and vinegar in a small bowl. Let stand for 5 minutes.

2 Combine the gluten-free flour, baking powder, and salt in a medium bowl.

3 Add the oil, syrup, and vanilla, if using, to the almond milk. Add to the dry ingredients and stir to blend.

4 Brush a preheated mini-waffle maker with vegan butter or spray with vegan nonstick cooking spray. Pour about ¼ cup batter into the waffle maker and cook according to the manufacturer's instructions. Remove with a silicone spatula and repeat with the remaining batter.

5 Serve warm with your favorite toppings, maple syrup, or vegan butter.

corn bread waffles

MAKES 8 MINI WAFFLES

This might be one of the most versatile waffles we've made. The cornmeal keeps the exterior of these golden waffles extra-crispy, which makes them perfect for munching straight up, layering on toppings, and standing in for bread on sandwiches. Just like traditional corn bread, they can be sweet or savory. Sweeten them up with a double dose of maple syrup or nudge them toward the savory Southwest with the addition of cheese and jalapeños.

¾ cup unbleached all-purpose flour
¾ cup yellow cornmeal
1 teaspoon baking powder
½ teaspoon baking soda
½ teaspoon sea salt
1 cup low-fat buttermilk
2 large eggs, lightly beaten
3 tablespoons unsalted butter, melted and cooled
1 tablespoon maple syrup

Melted butter or nonstick cooking spray, for the waffle maker

1. Combine the flour, cornmeal, baking powder, baking soda, and salt in a medium bowl.

2. Whisk the buttermilk, eggs, butter, and syrup in a small bowl. Add to the dry ingredients and stir to combine, without overmixing. Let the batter stand for 10 minutes.

3. Brush a preheated mini-waffle maker with melted butter or spray with nonstick cooking spray. Pour about ¼ cup batter into the waffle maker and cook according to the manufacturer's instructions. Remove with a silicone spatula and repeat with the remaining batter.

4. Serve warm with butter, maple syrup, or your preferred toppings.

VARIATIONS

For a sweeter waffle, add 1 more tablespoon maple syrup.

Blueberry Corn Bread Waffles: Gently fold ½ cup fresh blueberries into the batter.

Cheesy Corn Bread Waffles: Gently fold ½ cup coarsely grated cheddar cheese and 1 seeded and finely chopped small jalapeño (optional) into the batter.

whole-wheat pumpkin waffles

MAKES 8 MINI WAFFLES

A dollop of pumpkin purée adds the unmistakable whiff of autumn, and whole-wheat flour provides a toothsome edge to these fragrantly spiced waffles. If you like, add nuts to the batter for extra heft. Serve these waffles simply with butter and maple syrup, or go all out and garnish them with whipped cream and caramelized apples (page 42).

1 cup whole-wheat flour
1 teaspoon baking powder
½ teaspoon sea salt
½ teaspoon ground cinnamon
¼ teaspoon ground nutmeg
⅛ teaspoon ground cloves
¾ cup whole milk

2 large eggs, lightly beaten
3 tablespoons maple syrup
2 tablespoons unsalted butter, melted and cooled
1 teaspoon vanilla extract
¼ cup pumpkin purée

Melted butter or nonstick cooking spray, for the waffle maker

1. Combine the flour, baking powder, salt, cinnamon, nutmeg, and cloves in a medium bowl.

2. Whisk the milk, eggs, maple syrup, butter, and vanilla in a small bowl. Add to the dry ingredients and stir to combine. Gently fold in the pumpkin purée.

3. Brush a preheated mini-waffle maker with melted butter or spray with nonstick cooking spray. Pour about ¼ cup batter into the waffle maker and cook according to the manufacturer's instructions. Remove with a silicone spatula and repeat with the remaining batter.

4. Serve warm with maple syrup or your preferred toppings.

VARIATION

Pumpkin-Nut Waffles: Gently fold ¼ cup chopped walnuts or pecans into the batter with the pumpkin.

VARIATIONS

Banana-Nut Waffles: Gently fold ¼ cup chopped walnuts or pecans into the finished batter.

Banana–Chocolate Chip Waffles: Gently stir ½ cup chocolate chips into the finished batter.

banana waffles

MAKES 8 TO 10 MINI WAFFLES

We never say no to a pile of sliced bananas on top of a waffle, so why not indulge that banana hankering and mix them into the batter, too? You can still heap on the bananas before serving, preferably with a generous pour of maple syrup. If you want more bling, try adding chocolate chips, nuts, or shredded coconut to the batter. Just be sure to make a double batch, because these waffles are a perfect snack to pop into the toaster or stash in a lunch box.

1 cup unbleached all-purpose flour
½ cup whole-wheat flour
2 tablespoons sugar
1 teaspoon baking powder
½ teaspoon sea salt
½ teaspoon ground cinnamon
¾ cup whole milk
2 large eggs, lightly beaten
3 tablespoons unsalted butter,
  melted and cooled
½ teaspoon vanilla extract
1 large ripe banana, mashed

Melted butter or nonstick cooking spray,
  for the waffle maker

1 Combine the all-purpose flour, whole-wheat flour, sugar, baking powder, salt, and cinnamon in a medium bowl.

2 Whisk the milk, eggs, butter, and vanilla in a small bowl. Add to the dry ingredients and stir to combine. Gently fold in the banana.

3 Brush a preheated mini-waffle maker with melted butter or spray with nonstick cooking spray. Pour about ¼ cup batter into the waffle maker and cook according to the manufacturer's instructions. Remove with a silicone spatula and repeat with the remaining batter.

4 Serve warm with sliced bananas, maple syrup, or your preferred toppings.

egg mcwaffle **18**

frittaffle **20**

waffles with smoked salmon, lemon-chive cream cheese, and everything garnish **21**

grilled pimento cheese, tomato, and jalapeño waffle sandwiches **24**

bacon, lettuce, tomato, and avocado waffle sandwiches **26**

waffle joes **28**

twice-baked potato, cheese, and scallion waffles **30**

waffled panini with turkey, provolone, sun-dried tomatoes, and arugula **33**

waffled pizza margherita pockets **36**

fun

with

waffles

egg mcwaffle

MAKES 1 SANDWICH

There are some classics you should never mess with—except when waffles are involved. We did just that, and gave a little tweak to the beloved and iconic fast-food egg sandwich, substituting waffles, of course, for the muffin. In our humble opinion, they add just the right amount of dough and crispiness to our favorite breakfast sandwich. We think you'll agree.

2 savory waffles, such as Basic (page 3), Buttermilk (page 4), or Corn Bread (page 10)

Unsalted butter, room temperature

1 slice (1 ounce) cheddar, Monterey Jack, or American cheese, deli style, room temperature

Vegetable oil or nonstick cooking spray

1 large egg

Sea salt and freshly ground black pepper

1 slice Canadian bacon

Special equipment: 3-inch egg ring

1. Toast your waffles until golden. Lightly butter one side of both waffles and lay the cheese on the buttered side of one of the waffles.

2. In a small skillet with a lid, melt 1 teaspoon butter over medium heat. Brush the interior of the egg ring with vegetable oil or spray with nonstick cooking spray and place in the skillet. Crack the egg into the ring. Pierce the yolk with a fork so that it runs, and season the egg with salt and pepper. Cover the skillet with the lid (or another pan) and cook until the egg white is set, 3 to 4 minutes. Gently run a knife around the egg and remove the ring. Flip the egg and cook until the yolk is set, 1 to 2 more minutes. Lay the egg on top of the cheese.

3 Melt 1 teaspoon butter in the same skillet over medium heat. Fry the bacon in the butter until lightly browned, about 2 minutes. Place the bacon on top of the egg, then place the second waffle, buttered side down, over the bacon. Serve immediately.

frittaffle

Making a frittata couldn't be easier, quicker, or cuter. Instead of baking a pan-load of eggs in an oven, you can whip up a stack of mini frittatas in minutes. Be creative and have fun with this flexible recipe. Mix and match your favorite cheese and vegetables into the eggs—simply follow the amounts in this recipe. These frittaffles can be served warm or at room temperature.

½ tablespoon unsalted butter

½ cup deseeded and finely diced red bell pepper

¼ cup finely chopped yellow onion

½ cup chopped spinach

4 large eggs

2 tablespoons heavy cream

¼ cup finely grated Pecorino Romano cheese, plus extra for sprinkling

½ teaspoon sea salt

¼ teaspoon freshly ground black pepper

Melted butter or nonstick cooking spray, for the waffle maker

1 In a medium skillet, melt the butter. Add the pepper and onion and cook until soft, about 3 minutes, stirring frequently. Add the spinach and sauté until just wilted, about 1 minute. Remove from the heat.

2 Whisk the eggs, cream, the ¼ cup of cheese, the salt, and pepper in a medium bowl. Add the cooked vegetables and stir to combine.

3 Brush a preheated mini-waffle maker with melted butter or spray with nonstick cooking spray. Pour about ¼ cup egg mixture into the waffle maker and sprinkle with a pinch of cheese. Cook until golden brown and cooked through, 4 to 5 minutes. Remove with a silicone spatula and repeat with the remaining egg mixture. Serve warm or at room temperature.

waffles with smoked salmon, lemon-chive cream cheese, and everything garnish

MAKES 4 WAFFLES OR 8 HALVES

This is a perfect brunch platter. All of the garnishes and goodies that make up a deli-style smoked salmon and bagel plate converge on these waffles. Cut the waffles in half, pile on the toppings, and serve family style. The "everything garnish" mimics a bagel garnish, adding great flavor and pizzazz to the waffles.

CREAM CHEESE

6 ounces cream cheese, room temperature

2 tablespoons sour cream

1 teaspoon minced chives

½ teaspoon finely grated lemon zest

EVERYTHING GARNISH

1 teaspoon poppy seeds

1 teaspoon toasted sesame seeds

½ teaspoon finely grated lemon zest

¼ teaspoon coarse sea salt

¼ teaspoon coarsely ground black pepper

WAFFLES

4 savory waffles, such as Basic (page 3), Buttermilk (page 4), or Rise-and-Shine (page 6)

8 ounces smoked salmon, thinly sliced
½ small red onion, very thinly sliced, rings separated

2 teaspoons capers, rinsed

Dill sprigs

continued

1. Whisk the cream cheese ingredients until smooth and light. Set aside.

2. Combine the garnish ingredients in a small bowl and set aside.

3. Cook or toast the waffles until crisp.

4. Smear each waffle with 3 to 4 tablespoons of cream cheese and cut each waffle in half. Arrange the waffles on serving plates or a platter. Lay the salmon over the cream cheese. Top with rings of onion and the capers. Sprinkle the everything garnish over and around the waffles and top each waffle with a dill sprig. Serve right away.

grilled pimento cheese, tomato, and jalapeño waffle sandwiches

MAKES 4 SANDWICHES

Retro cheese spread meets trendy mini waffle, and it's a very happy union. Pimento cheese is enjoying a resurgence in our kitchens, and this recipe ratchets it up by smearing it between two toasted mini waffles with crisp and fresh jalapeño slices. Creamy, sweet, and piquant, this is guaranteed to satisfy any craving for an oozing toasted cheese sandwich.

PIMENTO CHEESE

4 ounces sharp cheddar cheese, finely grated

¼ cup drained jarred roasted red peppers or pimento, finely chopped

2 ounces cream cheese, softened

2 tablespoons mayonnaise, plus extra for toasting

½ teaspoon Worcestershire sauce

½ teaspoon hot sauce

¼ teaspoon sea salt

WAFFLES

8 Corn Bread Waffles (page 10)

1 to 2 jalapeño peppers, seeded, thinly sliced

4 large (center-cut) slices vine-ripened tomato, each about ¼ inch thick

1. Mix all of the pimento cheese ingredients together in a bowl until combined.

2. Spread a thin layer of mayonnaise on 1 waffle. Turn over and spread ¼ of the cheese on the other side of the waffle. Arrange 4 jalapeño slices over the cheese and top with a tomato slice. Spread a thin layer of mayonnaise on another waffle and cover the sandwich, mayonnaise side up. Repeat with the remaining waffles so that you have 4 sandwiches.

3. Preheat a large cast-iron skillet over medium heat. Place the sandwiches in the skillet. Toast over medium heat until the cheese begins to melt and the corn bread is golden brown, about 3 minutes. Flip the sandwiches and continue to toast until the cheese is melted and the corn bread is golden brown, 2 to 3 more minutes. Serve immediately.

bacon, lettuce, tomato, and avocado waffle sandwiches

MAKES 2 SANDWICHES

Can the classic BLT sandwich be perfected? We think so! We added thick slices of fresh avocado, generous smears of Sriracha-spiked mayonnaise, and—ahem—mini waffles to the usual recipe, and we think we have a winner. So go ahead and try this, and we'll let you be the judge.

1/4 cup mayonnaise

1 teaspoon Sriracha

4 savory waffles, such as Basic (page 3) or Corn Bread (page 10)

2 leaves lettuce, each about the size of a waffle

2 large (center-cut) slices vine-ripened tomato, each about 1/2 inch thick

4 slices thick-cut bacon, about 4 ounces, cooked until crisp

1/2 ripe avocado, cut into 1/4-inch slices

1 Whisk the mayonnaise and Sriracha in a small bowl. Set aside.

2 Toast the waffles until golden and crispy. Brush each waffle on one side with the mayonnaise.

3 Lay a lettuce leaf on the mayo side of 2 waffles and top each with a tomato slice. Arrange the bacon over the tomatoes and top with avocado. Close the sandwiches, mayo side down, with the remaining 2 waffles. Eat immediately.

waffle joes

MAKES 8 OPEN-FACE WAFFLES; SERVES 4

Yes, you can have waffles for dinner! The humble sloppy joe (a.k.a. timeless, family-friendly meal) gets a modern twist with the handy waffle stepping in for the burger bun. The corn bread waffles dutifully hold their shape, while their ridges capture the juices from the sweet and meaty sauce. Say goodbye to soggy burger buns—this spin-off is here to stay.

TOPPING

Extra-virgin olive oil

1 pound ground beef

½ small yellow onion, finely chopped, about ½ cup

½ small carrot, finely chopped, about ¼ cup

2 cloves garlic, minced

¼ teaspoon red pepper flakes

1 (15-ounce) can crushed tomatoes

⅓ cup ketchup

1 teaspoon Worcestershire sauce

1 teaspoon red wine vinegar

½ teaspoon dried thyme

1 teaspoon sea salt

¼ teaspoon freshly ground black pepper

WAFFLES

8 Corn Bread Waffles (page 10)

2 tablespoons chopped Italian parsley

1. Heat 1 tablespoon of oil in a skillet over medium heat. Add the meat and brown well, stirring occasionally, 8 to 10 minutes. With a slotted spoon, transfer the meat to a bowl.

2. Pour off all but 1 tablespoon of fat from the skillet (if the skillet is dry, add 1 tablespoon oil). Add the onion and carrot and sauté until softened, about 3 minutes. Add the garlic and red pepper flakes and sauté until fragrant, about 30 seconds.

3. Return the meat to the pan, add the tomatoes, ketchup, Worcestershire sauce, vinegar, thyme, salt, and pepper. Stir to combine. Simmer over medium-low heat for about 15 minutes.

4. Arrange the waffles on serving plates. Ladle the meat over the waffles, sprinkle with parsley, and serve immediately.

twice-baked potato, cheese, and scallion waffles

MAKES 10 (2½-INCH) POTATO CAKES

Who doesn't like a twice-baked potato, with its mashed-potato-and-creamy-cheese filling? We have a quick and crispy alternative to stuffing all of that cheesy potato goodness back into the skin. Simply form the filling into patties and crisp 'em on the waffle iron. For do-ahead prep, form the potato patties up to three hours in advance of cooking, cover with plastic wrap, and refrigerate. Let stand at room temperature for fifteen minutes before toasting.

2 large russet potatoes, about
   1½ pounds, baked and peeled,
   room temperature

½ cup (about 2 ounces) coarsely
   grated sharp cheddar cheese

¼ cup (2 ounces) cream cheese, softened

2 tablespoons sour cream, plus extra
   for dipping

1 scallion, white and green parts
   thinly sliced

1 garlic clove, minced or pushed through
   a press

1 teaspoon sea salt

½ teaspoon freshly ground black pepper

½ cup panko (Japanese bread crumbs),
   or more as needed

Melted butter or nonstick cooking spray,
   for the waffle maker

Fresh chives

continued

1. Combine the potatoes, cheddar cheese, cream cheese, the 2 tablespoons of sour cream, the scallion, garlic, salt, and pepper in a mixing bowl. Mash with a fork to blend.

2. Form the potatoes into ten 2-inch balls and slightly flatten into patties, about ½ inch thick. Pour the panko into a shallow bowl and lightly dredge the patties to achieve a thin coating.

3. Generously brush a preheated mini-waffle maker with melted butter or spray with nonstick cooking spray. Place a patty in the center of the waffle maker and toast until golden brown and crispy, about 5 minutes. Remove with a silicone spatula and repeat with the remaining patties. Garnish the potatoes with chives and serve warm with the sour cream for dipping.

4. The potato cakes may be kept warm in a 250°F oven while you are preparing the rest of the potatoes.

waffled panini with turkey, provolone, sun-dried tomatoes, and arugula

MAKES 2 PANINIS

Making panini couldn't be easier with a waffle iron. Use a 4-inch ring mold to form neat circles out of day-old brioche or challah bread, layer your favorite panini ingredients between two slices, and toast away in the waffle iron. Don't hold back, and experiment with your favorite panini ingredients. This is one of ours. We use the oil from a jar of sun-dried tomatoes to brush the outside of the sandwich before toasting, which helps to crisp and flavor the bread.

4 slices brioche or challah, each about ¼ inch thick

2 tablespoons sun-dried tomato oil

4 teaspoons Dijon mustard, divided

4 slices (4 ounces) roasted turkey, deli style

2 slices (2 ounces) provolone cheese, deli style

¼ cup drained and coarsely chopped oil-packed sun-dried tomatoes

½ cup loosely packed baby arugula

continued

1. Trim or cut the bread to the size of the waffle iron. Lightly brush 1 bread slice on one side with the sun-dried tomato oil. Spread about 1 teaspoon of mustard on the other side of the bread.

2. Lay 2 slices of turkey over the mustard side of the bread, folding or tearing to conform to the shape of the bread. Top with 1 slice of cheese, folding or tearing to conform to the shape of the bread. Top the cheese with half of the sun-dried tomatoes and half of the arugula.

3. Spread 1 teaspoon of mustard on a second bread slice and place, mustard side down, on the sandwich. Lightly brush the top with more tomato oil.

4. Place the sandwich in the waffle iron, close the lid, and firmly hold closed until the bread is toasted and the cheese melts, 4 to 5 minutes. Repeat with the remaining ingredients.

waffled pizza margherita pockets

MAKES 4 POCKETS

There are no limits to a waffle maker, including these plump pizza pockets you can also call mini calzones. Filled with tangy tomato sauce, fresh basil, and melty cheese, they are best enjoyed hot from the waffle maker. (Just remember to blow first!) When you make these, take care to gently press and not squeeze down on the waffle maker, or you may burst the pockets. Serve them straight up or with marinara sauce or basil pesto for dipping.

½ pound prepared pizza dough, divided into 4 equal balls

4 tablespoons marinara sauce, store-bought, plus more for dipping

4 tablespoons, about 2 ounces, coarsely grated mozzarella cheese

4 teaspoons, about 1 ounce, finely grated Parmesan cheese

4 to 8 large basil leaves

Extra-virgin olive oil

Basil pesto, for dipping

1   On a lightly floured surface, roll or stretch 1 dough ball into a circle about 4 inches in diameter.

2   Smear 1 tablespoon of sauce onto the dough, leaving a 1-inch border. Top with 1 tablespoon mozzarella, 1 teaspoon Parmesan, and 1 to 2 basil leaves.

3   Lift the edges of the dough up to the center and firmly pinch the dough closed. Gently press into a 2½ inch disk and seal. There should be no openings, or the filling will run out while cooking. Repeat with the remaining ingredients, making 4 total.

4 Brush a preheated mini-waffle maker with olive oil and place the pocket in the center. Gently close the top without squeezing the pocket. Toast until the dough is golden and firm, 4 to 5 minutes. Remove with a silicone spatula and brush the pocket on all sides with olive oil. Repeat with the remaining pockets.

5 Serve warm with marinara sauce or basil pesto for dipping, if desired.

desserts

with

waffles

strawberry short-waffles

MAKES 4 SERVINGS

We have taken the summer shortcake and layered it, naturally, with waffles. Luscious mascarpone is whipped into the heavy cream, giving structure and richness to the sumptuous layers, which makes it easier to pile on the toppings. We call this billowy berry bedecked waffle stack a dessert, but go on, you can have it for breakfast if you like. We won't tell.

⅔ cup heavy cream

⅓ cup mascarpone, room temperature

2 tablespoons sugar

¼ teaspoon vanilla extract

8 mini waffles, such as Basic (page 3), Buttermilk (page 4), or Rise-and-Shine (page 6)

1 pound fresh strawberries, hulled and halved (quartered if large)

Powdered sugar

Finely grated lemon zest

1 Beat the cream, mascarpone, sugar, and vanilla in a bowl with an electric mixer until soft peaks form.

2 Cook or reheat the waffles until crisp.

3 Arrange 4 waffles on individual serving plates. Spread a thick layer of cream over each waffle. Lightly press some of the strawberries into the cream and top with a second waffle. Sprinkle with powdered sugar and spoon a generous dollop of cream on top of each waffle stack. Scatter the remaining strawberries over and around the waffles. Garnish with the lemon zest. Serve immediately.

puff pastry waffles with caramelized apples and whipped cream

MAKES 8 SERVINGS

You can cook puff pastry on a waffle iron, and when you do, you'll never look back. Cut the pastry to fit the iron, sprinkle with a little sugar, and get toasting. In minutes, you will have crispy golden puff pastry. It's as easy as pie—and you'll be thinking of pie when you bite into these golden puff pastry waffles laden with cinnamon-spiced apples and whipped cream.

Special Equipment: 4-inch pastry ring

APPLES

¼ cup unsalted butter

½ cup sugar

4 Granny Smith apples, about 1½ pounds, cored, peeled, cut into ½-inch cubes

1 teaspoon cornstarch

½ teaspoon ground cinnamon

¼ teaspoon ground nutmeg

⅛ teaspoon sea salt

WAFFLES

1 sheet frozen puff pastry, thawed according to package instructions

2 tablespoons sugar

1 teaspoon cinnamon

Melted butter or nonstick cooking spray, for the waffle maker

Whipped cream

1. To make the apples, melt the butter in a skillet over medium-high heat. Add the sugar and heat until it begins to dissolve, about 2 minutes. Add the apples, cornstarch, cinnamon, nutmeg, and salt. Cook until the apples are tender and golden and the sauce has a thick syrup consistency, 6 to 8 minutes, stirring occasionally. Keep warm.

2. To make the waffles, unroll the puff pastry. Cut 8 (4-inch) circles out of the pastry with a pastry ring. Combine the sugar and cinnamon in a small bowl and sprinkle the pastry circles on both sides.

3. Brush a preheated mini-waffle maker with melted butter or spray with nonstick cooking spray. Lay a puff pastry circle on the waffle iron. Cook until puffed, golden, and crisp, about 4 minutes. Transfer to a wire rack and repeat with the remaining puff pastry.

4. Serve the puff pastry waffles topped with the apples and a dollop of whipped cream.

chocolate-dipped waffle pops

MAKES 32 SMALL WAFFLE POPS

Move over, cake pops—these waffle pops are fun, easy to make, and irresistible to eat. Almost any sweet waffle deserves to be dipped, so don't hold back with the flavors or toppings. We love the combination of chocolate and toasted almonds, but if you don't care for nuts, try a sprinkling of chopped toffee bars or candy sprinkles instead.

8 sweet waffles, such as Rise-and-Shine (page 6), Banana (page 15), or Brownie (page 46)

32 (4 to 6-inch) lollipop sticks

12 ounces high-quality semisweet chocolate chips

2 tablespoons vegetable shortening

1 cup unsalted almonds, toasted, chopped

1 Place a wire rack over a sheet of parchment paper. Quarter each waffle and insert a lollipop stick into each quarter.

2 Melt the chocolate and shortening in a double boiler over barely simmering heat, stirring until smooth.

3 Dip a waffle pop into the chocolate. Lay the waffle pop on the rack, with the stick weaving down through the rack grates, so the waffle is slightly raised.

4 Sprinkle with the nuts or your desired topping and let stand until set. Repeat with the remaining waffles.

brownie waffles
à la mode

MAKES 8 WAFFLES

Fellow chocoholics, this dessert is for you. A little bit brownie, a little bit cake, and all waffle, these chocolate babies are topped with vanilla ice cream, a drizzle of—gasp—more chocolate, and a shower of fresh raspberries for good measure. You're welcome.

¾ cup all-purpose flour

½ cup sugar

¼ cup unsweetened cocoa powder

1 teaspoon baking powder

½ teaspoon sea salt

2 large eggs, lightly beaten

⅓ cup heavy cream

¼ cup unsalted butter, melted and cooled

1 teaspoon vanilla extract

3 ounces semisweet chocolate mini
   morsels, about ½ cup

Melted butter or nonstick cooking spray,
   for the waffle maker

TOPPINGS

Vanilla ice cream

Chocolate sauce

Fresh raspberries

1 Combine the flour, sugar, cocoa powder, baking powder, and salt in a large bowl.

2 Whisk the eggs, cream, butter, and vanilla in a separate bowl. Add to the dry ingredients and fold in the mini morsels.

3 Brush a preheated mini-waffle maker with melted butter or spray with nonstick cooking spray. Pour about ¼ cup batter into the waffle maker and cook according to the manufacturer's instructions. Remove with a silicone spatula and repeat with the remaining batter.

4 Divide the waffles between serving plates. Top with a scoop of ice cream, the chocolate sauce, and raspberries.

metric conversions
and equivalents

APPROXIMATE METRIC EQUIVALENTS

Volume

¼ teaspoon	1 milliliter
½ teaspoon	2.5 milliliters
¾ teaspoon	4 milliliters
1 teaspoon	5 milliliters
1¼ teaspoon	6 milliliters
1½ teaspoon	7.5 milliliters
1¾ teaspoon	8.5 milliliters
2 teaspoons	10 milliliters
1 tablespoon (½ fluid ounce)	15 milliliters
2 tablespoons (1 fluid ounce)	30 milliliters
¼ cup	60 milliliters
⅓ cup	80 milliliters
½ cup (4 fluid ounces)	120 milliliters
⅔ cup	160 milliliters
¾ cup	180 milliliters
1 cup (8 fluid ounces)	240 milliliters
1¼ cups	300 milliliters
1½ cups (12 fluid ounces)	360 milliliters
1⅔ cups	400 milliliters
2 cups (1 pint)	460 milliliters
3 cups	700 milliliters
4 cups (1 quart)	0.95 liter
1 quart plus ¼ cup	1 liter
4 quarts (1 gallon)	3.8 liters

Weight

¼ ounce	7 grams
½ ounce	14 grams
¾ ounce	21 grams
1 ounce	28 grams
1¼ ounce	35 grams
1½ ounce	42.5 grams
1⅔ ounce	45 grams
2 ounces	57 grams
3 ounces	85 grams
4 ounces (¼ pound)	113 grams
5 ounces	142 grams
6 ounces	170 grams
7 ounces	198 grams
8 ounces (½ pound)	227 grams
16 ounces (1 pound)	454 grams
35.25 ounces (2.2 pounds)	1 kilogram

Length

⅛ inch	3 millimeters
¼ inch	6 millimeters
½ inch	1¼ centimeters
1 inch	2½ centimeters
2 inches	5 centimeters
2½ inches	6 centimeters
4 inches	10 centimeters
5 inches	13 centimeters
6 inches	15¼ centimeters
12 inches (1 foot)	30 centimeters

METRIC CONVERSION FORMULAS

To Convert	Multiply
Ounces to grams	Ounces by 28.35
Pounds to kilograms	Pounds by .454
Teaspoons to milliliters	Teaspoons by 4.93
Tablespoons to milliliters	Tablespoons by 14.79
Fluid ounces to milliliters	Fluid ounces by 29.57
Cups to milliliters	Cups by 236.59
Cups to liters	Cups by .236
Pints to liters	Pints by .473
Quarts to liters	Quarts by .946
Gallons to liters	Gallons by 3.785
Inches to centimeters	Inches by 2.54

OVEN TEMPERATURES

To convert Fahrenheit to Celsius, subtract 32 from Fahrenheit, multiply the result by 5, then divide by 9.

Description	Fahrenheit	Celsius	British Gas Mark
Very cool	200°	95°	0
Very cool	225°	110°	¼
Very cool	250°	120°	½
Cool	275°	135°	1
Cool	300°	150°	2
Warm	325°	165°	3
Moderate	350°	175°	4
Moderately hot	375°	190°	5
Fairly hot	400°	200°	6
Hot	425°	220°	7
Very hot	450°	230°	8
Very hot	475°	245°	9

COMMON INGREDIENTS AND THEIR APPROXIMATE EQUIVALENTS

1 cup uncooked white rice = 185 grams

1 cup all-purpose flour = 140 grams

1 stick butter (4 ounces • ½ cup • 8 tablespoons) = 110 grams

1 cup butter (8 ounces • 2 sticks • 16 tablespoons) = 220 grams

1 cup brown sugar, firmly packed = 225 grams

1 cup granulated sugar = 200 grams

Information compiled from a variety of sources, including *Recipes into Type* by Joan Whitman and Dolores Simon (Newton, MA: Biscuit Books, 1993); *The New Food Lover's Companion* by Sharon Tyler Herbst (Hauppauge, NY: Barron's, 2013); and *Rosemary Brown's Big Kitchen Instruction Book* (Kansas City, MO: Andrews McMeel, 1998).

index

mini-waffle cookbook

Andrews McMeel Publishing
a division of Andrews McMeel Universal
1130 Walnut Street, Kansas City, Missouri 64106

www.andrewsmcmeel.com

18 19 20 21 22 SHO 10 9 8 7 6 5 4 3 2

ISBN: 978-1-4494-8983-0

Library of Congress Control Number: 2017942401

Editor: Jean Lucas
Photography: Lynda Balslev
Art Director: Holly Swayne
Production Editor: Maureen Sullivan
Production Manager: Carol Coe

Cover photo © StockFood/Great Stock!
Page vi © Getty/MarkGillow; page 2 © Getty/eddieberman;
page 11 © Getty/etienne voss; page 14 © Getty/Pannonia

attention: schools and businesses

Andrews McMeel books are available at quantity discounts with bulk purchase for educational, business, or sales promotional use. For information, please e-mail the Andrews McMeel Publishing Special Sales Department: specialsales@amuniversal.com.